ACKNOWL1

My thanks go to the publishing, printing and marketing professionals who have helped me to produce this Anthology.

There are many who will be unaware that they have helped me since some of the poems have relied upon observation rather than interaction with others. My thanks go to these unknown individuals.

In other cases the poems have been written specifically for friends and family and my thanks go to them. (You know who you are!)

Furthermore my family have been a constant support during the preparation of this Anthology. However special thanks go to my wife Libby whose administrative skills and eye for detail have kept me on track. She has also been a sounding board for ideas and someone who I can rely upon for useful feedback.

FOREWORD

As a bookseller and owner of Serendip books in Lyme Regis, I was pleased to be approached by Geoff to write a Foreword for his poetry anthology.

Geoff has the ability to write poems spanning a wide range of emotions. One of his talents is to offer poetry in an entertaining and uplifting way, while at the same time challenging the reader.

The poems have universal appeal and can be enjoyed by people from nine to ninety-nine! Recently Geoff read some of his poetry to a sell-out audience as part of the Lyme Regis ArtsFest. I am looking forward to having his book on my shelves, for amongst the pages there are many real gems.

Bee Painton
Serendip

PREFACE

From 1997 I have suffered from Parkinson's Disease. Whether it is as a result of the disease itself, the drugs taken or other factors, negative aspects of Parkinson's have been accompanied by an ability to write poetry.

Shortly after I was diagnosed I experienced a major outpouring of verses often written at night and at speed: a speed which suggested that they had been queuing and waiting for their release into daylight. As a result, characters such as Young Mr Dibble and Shootalinus the Ticket Tout were born. Now the queues are shorter but the writing continues! It struck me that at least some of this ability might be found in my genes inherited from my Great-Grandfather and his son my Grandfather who were entertainers and illusionists. They both used the stage name 'Dr Lynn' and the former is credited with inspiring Houdini.

There comes a time when one has to decide just what to do with 200 poems! I have chosen a cross-section of 50 for this anthology. I was keen that their flavour should be reflected in the book's title hence it is called *Poetic Stuff and Nonsense*. I want this collection to entertain and enrich a wide audience.

CONTENTS

POETIC STUFF AND NONSENSE

SHEEPISH

"Would you say I'm sheepish?"
Said Marion to Jane
Jane said "It's our destiny
From which we can't refrain
Being sheepish is our calling
We do not have a choice
We might as well stop stalling
Be sheepish with one voice
To pull the wool over your eyes
And say that we are not
Would serve no useful purpose
Would not achieve a lot
Our work with those insomniacs
Also deserves a mention
Although to take this work on
Was never our intention
Displaying other qualities
Would not suit a sheep
So now we are accounted for
Let's try and get some sleep!"

LIONEL NO LONGER SPOTLESS

Lionel was a smart young leopard
One who liked to work and play hard
Got on well with his relations
Although there were some limitations
One thing disturbing him and others
Teenage friends, sisters and brothers
Was that as poor Lionel grew
Spots did not come into view
Now as you know, leopards have spots
I haven't seen one that does not
But sadly in poor Lionel's case
No spots appeared, just lots of space
He asked his parents whether they
From memory might or may
Have had a spotless old relation
Which might explain his situation
His parents could not answer 'yes'
And all were suffering from stress
His parents were at their wit's end
They didn't know just where to send
Poor Lionel, but with lateral thinking
They had a plan to stop him sinking
Saying the way they could assist
Was to go to a Pharmacist…

So they went to their local Boots
For spot enhancer that would suit
The problem that poor Lionel had
They really tried to help the lad
The leopards hunted high and low
But spot enhancer failed to show
For all the products they could find
(and this completely blew their minds)
Removed spots, not the opposite
They'd failed, they had now to admit
The others who were serving there
Were clearly very well aware
Of Lionel's desperate situation
And without much hesitation
Offered help, 'now please don't stop
You'll find the answer in the shop
Next door, the owner there will tell you more'
They rushed to the adjacent store
Explained the problem and some more
About poor Lionel's current state
'Please help us now or it's too late'
The owner just said 'please don't worry
We can do this in a hurry
We do stripes and spots and stars
The very best in town by far...

Tigers, zebras, ring-tailed monkeys
Those who just want to look funky
All you do is paint spots on
Their rain resistant', whereupon
He applied a great design
And Lionel shouted, 'It's all mine
Now as a leopard I feel fine
Spots are subtly out of line
Making me much more unique
He's given me the look I seek'
So now young Lionel jumped for joy
No longer spotless, feeling coy
'Now I'm spotty, what a blast
A personal set of spots at last
My teenage friends will count me in
I've even got spots on my chin!'

HARDLY PANDA-MONIUM

He pandered to her constantly
But she was quite detached
This left people wondering –
Perhaps they weren't well matched?
She hadn't had a photograph
Or any information
A hit and miss affair it seems –
No previous commendation
Therefore the chances of success
Did not seem that great
Since the female of the species
Was indifferent to her mate
Was it a change in climate?
Or could it be the food?
Perhaps it was the tourists?
For hours many had queued
Hoping for some action
Most left not having viewed
And even those who waited
Said that nothing much ensued!

TIME TO GO?

Come on Cedric, time to go
We've been here long enough, you know
Most residents are ninety plus
And keep on going without fuss
Or bother to the nursing staff
Sharing the occasional laugh
We know that we get nursing care
Immediate access, always there
Lives prolonged but one asks why
We're on prescription 'til we die
And when like salmon we must leap
Retreating into permanent sleep
Our name is removed from the door
No record of who went before
I think it's time for you and me
To go now…

So we're back for tea
Be thankful our mobility
And the Pub's proximity
Allow us both to break the rules
Like schoolboys bunking off from school
And with care escape detection
What chance of permanent defection?

A CASE OF MISTAKEN IDENTITY

"Pullover" said the Policeman
"Do you like it?" said young Fred
"I bought it at the Co-op
They come in blue and red
They do it with a V-neck
Or turtle neck instead
If you think that it's good quality
It is quite cheap" said Fred
"Pullover" said the Policeman
Fred said "what can I say?
Washing instructions indicate
It will not shrink or fray
It is the perfect pullover
It has a certain style
I'm pleased to say to own one
Doesn't have to cost a pile"
"Pullover" said the Policeman
Fred twigged and then complied
So they both pulled over
And then the Policeman cried
"Next time I say 'pullover'
Please move over straight away
Your sleeve's caught in the door jam
Driving's dangerous that way…

When I say 'pullover'
Please listen carefully
The message was indeed about
Your pullover you see
But first you have to pullover
I hope that this is clear
Next time I say pullover
Please just do it – do you hear?"

LOVE SICK LILY

She sat there every Sunday
In the middle of row one
She never missed a sermon
Come rain or snow or sun
When the collection plate came round
She always put coins in
Often they were foreign ones
Places her brother'd been
If the vicar smiled at her
She'd blush and go quite crimson
And when she did wear glasses
That she'd bought
With metal rims on
Tears just flowed across the lenses
Enough to float a boat on
Her tear ducts were prolific
And with moisture down her face
She also sobbed a little
brought a hanky just in case!
Sadly tittle-tattle said
That Lily's rather simple
Her one redeeming feature
Was she had a double dimple
Nobody really knew her
Because she never spoke...

As a result she was the butt
Of other people's jokes
When the service finished
And people left the church
She'd linger, slip her hand in his
Until the vicar's search
For someone else to say goodbye to…
Offered a release
At least until the next time
Since her handshakes never ceased
One day the Parish News announced
"Your vicar's moving on
A bigger Parish beckons
In a few weeks he'll be gone"
After this announcement
She never came again
The front pew was still filled
By others even when it rained
The new vicar was unaware
Of Lily's 'liaison'
For now her love affair had died
Her lover had moved on!

IN THE PINK

Pink elephants are rather rare
Accounting for why people stare
If they bump into one by chance
It's bound to get a second glance
Seeing is believing so they say
But people's mindsets say we're grey
So meeting one who's in the pink
Presents more challenge than you'd think
Since unicorns and pigs that fly
Pole vaulting cows that jump moon high
Are all employed as you will see
To help people think laterally
You may not ever see a yeti
Or a tree that grows spaghetti
But I say don't be deterred
If you find us then spread the word
Outside the box imagination
Is important for creation
If all our elephants were grey
Life could be rather dull we say!

HATS THAT MATTER

You must be mad to wear that hat
It helps, I said, as a matter of fact
I've got a lot more hats at home
From city gent to garden gnome
I wore a bowler on the train
From Coulsdon South and back again
With brolly, briefcase and dark suit
Performing a faceless commute
My boater was a special hat
Just made from straw – no worse for that
I felt that it would serve to flatter
When I attended a Regatta
So many shapes, so many sizes
So many hats to aid disguises
Moleskin, rabbit, kangaroo
Or paper hats just stuck with glue
Remember hats will always matter
At parties given by the Hatter
Don't worry if your hat's bizarre
To come without one's worse by far!

TOADS IN A HOLE

Somebody said "Toads cross here"
Were they upset? It wasn't clear
When I enquired about cross toads
They said that motorists had not slowed
And casualties amongst the toads
Meant they were cross and anger showed
For this migration was for mating
With the toads anticipating
Pleasures further down the line
But right now there was no sign
Any less adventurous toad
Concerned about crossing the road
Said "It's a risk, it's not for me
So I'll opt for celibacy!"
The rest said "Let's get signs installed"
And most of them said "We're appalled
That cars aren't watching out for toads
Who regularly cross the roads!"
Toads felt they didn't get fair treatment
Despite the e-mails they had sent
To those responsible for roads
Who in the main ignored the toads
Zebras, Pelicans and Pandas
All got crossings that were grander...

These included flashing lights
Alerting cars both day and night
With time the toads became quite sore
Since their file still said "ignore"
So they conducted wild cat strikes
All toad work stopped both day and night
When cones came out in sympathy
Toads found almost immediately
They got their way; signs were erected
But the toads remained dejected
Because to their immense dismay
Though signs gave a bold display
Camouflage and the toads' small size
Still often led to their demise!

FISHWIFE'S LAMENT

Being a fishwife's not much fun
With boats passed down from Dad to Son
Although I always wash their clothes
A fishy smell sticks in my nose
And when at night I dream in bed
I cuddle up to a mackerel's head
With oily skin and fishy smell
It clearly doesn't auger well
For love life it spells doom and gloom
I think I'll sleep in the other room!

REGGIE – A STUDY IN HORSEPLAY

Here are two extracts from a series of poems about a retired racehorse called Reggie...

UNSTABLE REGGIE

Reggie staggered home one night
He'd been out on the tiles
His hooves were really hurting
It seemed he'd walked for miles
He'd been out with old Ronnie
Who was the senior horse
They'd missed the coach and horses home
Through drunkenness, of course
They'd visited a nightclub
With young fillies who were coarse
They were the 'Weston-Super-Mares'
A special breed of horse!
Who gave them both a mud bath
Leading later to remorse
Although at the time
It was enjoyable, of course
After this experience
The duo couldn't pay
When finally they left for home
They couldn't find their way
Reggie couldn't see straight
And fell down on the floor
Ronnie fell on top of him
And both began to snore…

By morning they'd both staggered up
And swayed back to the yard
Questioned about their antics
They found recall quite hard
They remembered that the 'Super-Mares'
Had given them a bath
But after that their memories failed
There was no aftermath
The stud owner was quite upset
She'd seen it all before
Would Reggie ever change his ways?
She'd let him try once more!

REGGIE PUTS ON THE RITZ

One occasion which vexed Martha
Whilst in London with partner Arthur
Who allegedly trained horses –
More used to pubs than to race courses –
Was whilst they had tea at The Ritz
She paid; Arthur was thrilled to bits
She'd just devoured her third cream cake
Probably a big mistake
A handicap linked to The Ritz
Pity the horse on which she sits
The pianist was about to play
But now there was a short delay
The silence broken by a scuffle
Some would call it a kerfuffle
At the centre of the din
Was Reggie
They wouldn't let him in!
For he was both jacket and tieless
Accompanied by one he called 'My Lass'
One of the Weston-Super-Mares
Involved in photo booth affairs
Martha was by now quite harassed
Did not want to be embarrassed
Said "I'll vouch for the horse and filly…

I'm sure they'll recognise they're silly
To have made a fuss
Is there a tie that he can borrow
We'll send it back all clean tomorrow?"
The manager then hesitated
Thinking he might be berated
By other guests hard to convince
Just the thought made him wince
Saying "yes" just spelled disaster
For neither of them could master
The cutlery laid on the table
Both used to food served in their stable
Jam and cream flew everywhere
And everybody stood and stared
At Reggie and his female friend
Would they reach a sticky end?
At this point Martha's eyes made contact
With the manager; she had to act
Ordered a horsebox straight away
Despite Reggie's emphatic "Neigh"
Whisked the equine pair away
In doing so she saved the day
Would Reggie ever get it right?
It's clear he hadn't seen the light!

THE SHED

Don't shed a tear
The timber's here
As panels for assembly
It shouldn't take us quite as long
As it took rebuilding Wembley
It comes complete with nails and screws
Of different shapes and sizes
Before we start we'll have to check
Just what the bag comprises
Like many flat packs this one comes
With notes on what to do
And when in doubt use common sense
A gift possessed by few!
Bit by bit the panels fit
Well, nearly one might say
With angles fairly accurate
Once screwed together it should stay
Construction workers laboured long
Some harder than others
But in the end the three emerged
A sweaty band of brothers!
And now it's time for topping out
The final task for us
We've put this shed together
With the minimum of fuss!

THE ART OF PERSUASION

Well, old cock, I'm here again
And as before I will sustain
My hit rate as a hunting dog fox
Better check your bolts and deadlocks
On that ill-fitting henhouse door
For you're about to lose some more
Hens, and the farmer won't be pleased
I really like to see him teased
And with my nose right to the ground
My informants, who are sound
Say hens are not a happy bunch
Not just because they might make lunch
They say you've lost your 'cock-a-doodle'
Do you agree you're not now useful
Retirement, you cannot resist
Because the farmer will insist
That you are now an overhead
As such you might as well be dead
So open up the henhouse door
For life is more than hens and perches
This is confirmed by my researches
Yes, open up and fly away
As dawn breaks please don't delay
I'll tidy up
Is that OK?!

THE REPRIEVE

Maureen was a Jersey cow (and a music fanatic)
She wore an i-pod round her neck
And she was rarely static
Dancing round the field all day
While the sun shone she made hay
And as she danced she sang along
With perfect pitch, so rarely wrong
And every day at milking time
The i-pod on button would shine
She liked the big hits from the past
And from her collection, which was vast
A group called ABBA was her choice
Since their songs suited her voice
The vocal range was right for her
And friends who listened did concur
One day she heard the farmer say
"It's to the abattoir today"
Now Maureen could remember when
She learnt some French from a small hen
At least she could count up to ten!
This led her to the false conclusion
Enabling bovine delusion
That ABBA were now down to three
Needed a fourth – "It could be me"
She said, and was elated…

But it wasn't what the farmer stated
These thoughts did not make her calmer
Instead they were to trigger drama
At noon a cattle truck arrived
To take the cattle for a ride
From which they would not now return
The farmer didn't look concerned
Poor Maureen jostled with the rest
She knew a window seat was best!
For her, was this the final curtain?
A betting man would say for certain
But as she stood there in the queue
With i-pod on – nothing to do
She sang along to ABBA's music
Causing the owner's ears to prick
"What a voice that Jersey cow has
Listen to the razzamatazz
An abattoir with ABBA songs
Sung by a cow – there will be throngs
Of people – what a scene
Maureen, a cow, sings Dancing Queen"
So he bought her from the farmer
Thus avoiding beefsteak drama
Maureen then became a star
Twice daily at the abattoir!

GIFT OF THE CAB

Why do some London cabbies
Seem to do a lot of talking?
Are they lonely in the front
As they drive Heathrow to Dorking?
In general they're a genial bunch
Their backgrounds are diverse
If you value conversation
You could do a lot worse
But remember that the 'knowledge'
Is not just one-way streets
It's all the information
That they glean from those rear seats!

THE WING THREE-QUARTER
(REFLECTIONS OF A SCHOOL BOY)

There are those who will attest
I used to have to wear a vest
Although I'd vehemently protest
My dear old Mother thought it best
Pursuing my health care with zest
When playing games others would jest
Why has he got his thermals on?
Even when the sun had shone
The worst time was the winter team games
Standing shivering, being called names
A wing three-quarter with a vest
Really couldn't look his best
Dear old Mum, I tried to tell her
I didn't look good in Viyella!

TROUBLE AT THE FROG AND SPROCKET

I met a tree frog recently
Who was dressed quite indecently
He had a waistcoat of bright green
The like of which I'd never seen
But wasn't wearing any trews
It seems that he was bound to lose
"Why are you scantily attired?"
The tearful frog said he'd been fired
Trews were part of the uniform
With shirt and tie so he'd conform
To other staff within the Pub
At this point he began to blub
"They fired me without rightful cause
Breaching the clear contractual clause
Stating I had the right to wear
My waistcoat and they wouldn't care
Punters complained it was too bright
Especially when it caught the light
The boss said 'you cannot survive'
And gave me my P45
'We'll fire you from the Frog and Sprocket
Even though it hits your pocket
We can't have customers at night
Being affected by the light...

The waistcoat caused a strobe effect
That many punters could detect
Resulting in continuous blinking
Accompanied by a lack of drinking'
They then removed my hired clothing
Causing Frog and Sprocket loathing
Because they left me almost nude
Which those (not in the know) thought rude
I think both Pub and I will lose
And right now I've got no trews!"

INTERNAL DIALOGUE

How shall I deal with Josephine?
She's come in late again
She's done it now for several weeks
I wish that she'd refrain
I guess I should have tackled it
When I became aware
And having left it all this time
It's become a nightmare!
I'm feeling much embarrassment
Since my procrastination
Has led her to continue
With her unhelpful action
Others in the team are cross
And I am at a loss
Suppose I'd better talk to her
Now that I'm the boss!

LESS THAN LUCKY

Among the many rabbits
Who have been given life
There was one we called Magic
As sharp as any knife
He could perform illusions
A dozen, maybe more
And unlike other rabbits
He really knew the score
His home was in a black top hat
For which he paid no rent
As long as he kept smiling
And never showed dissent
He'd been sawn up so many times
His mind had become split
His expertise with jigsaws
Ensured each piece would fit
He'd disappear from cabinets
Escape from secure trunks
Remove several locked padlocks
You could hear the levers clunk
As he learned the combination
So he could then escape
Recording all the moves he made
Onto video tape…

Unfortunately one fateful day
When trying something new
Attempts to catch a bullet
With the aid of superglue
Went wrong before the gun was fired
His mouth and nose got stuck
So Magic met a sticky end
He ran right out of luck!

DOLLY: A PARISIAN DRAMA

Dolly had a special dress
It had polka dots no less
The spots were green
The background white
She really was a pretty sight
Her accessories it's said
Were by contrast brightest red
Expensive hat and scarf and shoes
You'd think that she just could not lose
But she had lived above her means
In Paris since her early teens
And her view of liquidity
Was how much vodka she
Could reasonably consume
On one occasion
She didn't need that much persuasion!
"I like a drink" she'd often say
"That doesn't mean I need AA"
But having reached aged twenty-three
For friends it was quite plain to see
That she was plastered by lunch-time
Sufficiently that when she climbed
Into the backseat of a car…
Accompanied by "her friend" vodka
She was unsteady on her feet…

And friends were not so keen to meet her
As she could become quite rude
When alcohol controlled her mood
In time, it seems, all doors had closed
Poor Dolly was, for sure, exposed
At this point she first met Pierre
With bulging biceps and black hair
He could see she was in a state
And would need help if to relate
To him instead of alcohol
Which had, by now, taken its toll
He gave support and much attention
At last she signed for intervention
The clinic's regime wasn't easy
But she persevered and could see
Light beyond the vodka bottle
Switching off the spirit's throttle
Pierre was there by her side
Helping her to turn the tide
Something he did not find hard
Since he was a young lifeguard
Who rescued Dolly from the Seine
They say it won't happen again
She'd slipped and fallen so we're told
He'd pulled her out shivering and cold
Now reunited they were wed
Her special dress looked great it's said
And young Pierre had thought it best
To wear a smart new lifeguard vest!

A PIG TALE FOR EASTER

Lambs that frolic
Chicks that cheep
Bunnies from their burrows leap
These are signs that Easter's here
New life in view it would appear
Commercially it seems quite clear
A great time for the Chocolatier
Edible art we can enjoy
Feast our eyes and then destroy
With excuses to indulge
Even though our stomachs bulge
New born creatures centre stage
Chicks and bunnies all the rage
So why do piglets get left out
Don't get a look in tail to snout
Is it because they grunt don't cheep?
Or unlike lambs they do not leap
And frolic in the spring-like air
Constrained by trotters – hardly fair!
Piglets would find it fulfilling
To enjoy parallel billing
Hopefully with little tension
Achieved without undue dissension
Chocolate pigs would then appear
Sculpted by the Chocolatier!

ME-ANDERS

It's not that easy being me
Who am I? Can I really see?
Am I the me that you can see
Or someone else to a degree
And is the me that I'm aware of
Like the one you have a share of
Or am I in reality
Not the one you or I see?
Again I ask so who am I
What is the truth and what's a lie?
So what is real and what is not
Did I know once and then forgot
Illusions lodged in people's minds
Until they are completely blind
And so we live life thinking we
Are free to choose
But in reality
For many it's a fantasy
Viewed through eyes that
Cannot see!

DIBBLE, A HARE WITH STYLE

Dibble was my first poetic partner! It seemed that every time I sat down to write, he was there. Here are four poems with Dibble as the central character...

NO MORE NECK NIBBLING

Young Mr Dibble
Persistently nibbled
The neck of his new neighbour's wife
The neighbour said 'hop it'
But he couldn't stop it
For Dibble the nibble was rife!

I don't want to quibble
With you Mr Dibble
But nibbling has just got to stop
Since I have seen it
To show that I mean it
If you don't stop you'll be for the chop!

This thought troubled Dibble
Who had one last nibble
Then finally gave up the chase
Now the neighbour's delighted
His wife's neck's not blighted
Since Dibble the chop couldn't face!

But what of poor Dibble
Now he cannot nibble
The neck of his new neighbour's wife
He has kicked the habit
He's dating a rabbit
And having the time of his life!

AROMATHERAPY

Hare Dibble, famous for neck nibbling
Kicked the habit after quibbling
From the neighbour most affected
For a while he was dejected

At first he really missed the habit
Then he began dating a rabbit
Initially things went quite well
Until he noticed a strong smell

From whence it came he couldn't tell
Although it did not auger well
For his rabbit relationship
At best it caused passion to slip

After a while he realised
When he'd had time to analyse
What caused this unpleasant aroma
It clearly wasn't a misnomer

The rabbit's home was underground
With limited fresh air around
She lived down there with several rabbits
Many with poor washing habits!

By contrast, Dibble, our young hare
Lived above ground, in open air
And now the smell dampened his ardour
Sufficiently that it was harder…

For him to make close advances
Or to try romantic dances
At last it all came to a head
The rabbit Dibble could not wed

Rabbit dating's not for me
And I'm afraid, reluctantly,
I'll seek a partner, who I know
Doesn't suffer from BO!

DINING DANGEROUSLY

Hare Dibble hadn't got a mate
And was concerned it was too late
It left him wondering what comes next
He was quite naturally perplexed
Let's hope that this young Casanova
Given time to think things over
Will make a better fist of it
Than in the past so flames are lit
Whilst he was thinking, it is said
Late at night and in his bed
As he lay there reviewing choices
He imagined he heard voices
He listened and it was a bird
Which Dibble clearly had misheard
He thought it said "the wit to woo"
And that advice on what to do
Might be forthcoming from this source
It was a wise old owl, of course
But rather than giving advice
To hares rolling the dating dice
He was out hunting for some food
And Dibble had mistaken woo'd
Thinking that it referred to dating
And thus provided help with mating...

So he hailed the bird in flight
Rather in the way you might
Hail a taxi, flag it down
To get yourself a lift in town
For Dibble this was a mistake
The bird was clearly out to take
A fast food option at a drive-in
So could Dibble stay alive in
Circumstances such as these
Trembling profusely at the knees
He engaged the wise old owl
Rather than throw in the towel
Good news – tonight he was in luck
The owls food order came unstuck
"Double rabbit burger please
With a topping of blue cheese"
Dibble mindful of his plight
Said "due to an oversight
No rabbit burgers left tonight
When we've restocked come for a bite
You've really come in rather late
What's left is passed its sell by date"
With that the owl t'wit t'woo'd
In fact what he said was quite rude
He flew off to a local diner
Which served young rabbits
– nothing finer!
Tasty youngsters who had strayed…

Across the road and they had paid
A heavy price for poor map reading
As meals for owls who do need feeding
So Dibble knew he had been lucky
Although fair do's, he had been plucky
Next time he hears "t'wit t'woo"
At least he'll know what NOT to do!

WISE WORDS
FOR THE WATERFORD GNOME

As Hare Dibble grew and grew
He stumbled upon something new
A hare extension, quite bizarre
Developed from his own sofa
Showing that success today
Comes to those who are au fait
With hardware, software and e-bay
As a result he now was rich
No longer living near the ditch
On waste ground and close by the fence
A millionaire in every sense
He set his sights on helping others
Rewarding all like-minded brothers
With advice to get them started
With wise words before they parted
So on a Wednesday every week
He gave up time to take a peek
At those who queued outside his home
First up was a garden gnome
Who'd come from Waterford, no less
He was so desperate for success
He'd brought his special fishing tool
Which he developed whilst at school...

But all this time there'd been no interest
So would Dibble care to invest?
Because now at age fifty-four
His confidence had hit the floor
The gnome explained "the tool's for fishing
And assists gnomes who are wishing
To cast their lines across the water
But because they are much shorter
Than the average fisherman
Need some help so that they can
So if you're under two foot three
You'd have no trouble then, you see
In fact you could fish normally"
He demonstrated perfectly
The gnome asked Dibble for advice
Our hare did not have to think twice
"It may be that your target group
Is wrongly chosen for this scoop
How many gnomes, would you agree
Are under about two foot three?"
Focussing hard on the question
The gnome looked glum after digestion
He said "well thinking carefully
The only one I know is me"
So Dibble had unlocked the issue…

And handing him a man-sized tissue
Said "I don't want to besmirch
Any of your own research
But it seems that it was flawed
Otherwise you should have scored
The product's good it should sell well
But need and product just don't gel
The concept's great it's really fine
But gnomes are about two foot nine
And some are even taller still"
So it was a bitter pill
Our watery gnome now had to swallow
Poor research had seem him wallow
He now could see, for forty years
He'd been six inches in arrears!

AGA SAGA

"I'd rather like an Aga"
Said Josephine to Don
"It's chilly in the kitchen
And an Aga when switched on
Would generate sufficient heat
For temperatures to rise
No need for chunky pullovers
As a compromise
But now we have to make a choice
Gas, Oil or Solid Fuel?
Don't forget Electric –
More expensive as a rule –
But with more investigation
Electric Aga wins
It meets all our criteria
So the rest can now be binned
Our three oven monster
Is really quite exciting
Though learning how to work it all
At first may seem quite frightening
And finally a colour –
Red, Blue, Green, Cream or White
We'll go for cream
Fulfil our dream
It's going to look just right
So now we can join Aga folk
And go to Aga parties
They'll tell us ours was a good choice
We've become Aga Smarties!"

LOOKING FOR A PURR-FECT LIFE

Who am I?
I'm not sure yet
It really is quite hard
Is what I see reality
Or just a facade?
Can you know other people
Before you know yourself?
It seems many will walk through life
With truth left on the shelf
I'd like to think life's simple
But plainly it is not
The maps we have to steer us through
Don't always help us plot
A path that is appropriate
But then just what is that?
If I come back another time
Perhaps I'll be a cat
A pampered pet with food laid on
And entertainment too
And of course I'll have nine lives
I'd like that wouldn't you?

TOBY'S TALE... AS A DOG

"It's snowing and they're going out
I wonder what that's all about?
On reflection, I don't care
I've spied a bag – there's food in there!
The chocolates could be for me
Organic!" he said gleefully
"If I'm quick and scoff the lot
The fact they've gone they may not spot"
Anne now stepped out from the bath
And surveyed the aftermath
Suffice to say there was a mess
Who was to blame? Well you can guess!
By now Toby felt quite unwell
One look at him and you could tell
So he was now rushed to the Vet
Where Anne would pay the doggy debt
The party scuppered by the dog
Though Toby when he wrote his blog
Did not mention Anne's night out
Chocolates first – there was no doubt!

THE SLEEPING BEAUTY

Have you met Patina?
She's been hiding in the grain
Waiting for the moment
When she can live again
She was no longer fashionable
And her pleas were in vain
Caresses went to others
Since she was on the wane
They marched her to a darkened room
A damp, foul smelling cellar
Would the sentence be for life
In solitary for ever?
But one day a shaft of light
Announced an opening door
How long had she been sleeping
A hundred years or more?
Patina didn't look her best
But those who entered saw
That underneath
Patina would look better than before
A little restoration to help Patina shine
And everyone who saw her
Said "I wish that she was mine"
For she now had an elegance…

Not possible when new
Her beauty was not just skin deep
It penetrated through
And clearly she'd improved with age
As many of us do!
The subtlety of colour
The texture of the wood
Impossible to replicate
Although some wish they could!

SEE SEA LION INSIDE

I had a sea lion for my birthday
It didn't fit into the bath
I had to send it to Newfoundland
It was sent to me for a laugh

They shipped it on to Baffin Island
And it protested all the way
It thought that it had bought a ticket
From Serengeti to LA

So it was not your usual sea lion
It was a lion who sought the sea
His objective to go surfing
On the west coast preferably

He got unpacked in Baffin Island
And took his surf-board from the hold
He tried to swap it for a bob sleigh
No call for surf-boards – far too cold!

So by this time he was quite angry
And ate the pilot and the crew
Since he had been so close to starving
Then he ate his surf-board too!

So if you do receive a parcel
And it is marked "See lion inside"
Don't jump too quickly to conclusions
For the label's just a guide…

It may indeed be a sea lion
But if you find that it is not
Don't send it off to Baffin Island
Because to post it costs a lot!

TEMPORARY CUSTODY LISTING BADLY

"So you are Grade II listed?"
The house said "Yes, that's right
They love my timber framing
And my ceiling height
I'm suitably impractical
With draughty inglenooks
Which aren't quite as idyllic
As those described in books!
I've got an ageing cesspit
It doesn't work too well
And so in the hot weather
There is a nasty smell!
Floors slope in all directions
You have to hold on tight
And once you've had a glass of wine
It's hard to stay upright!
Dampness occurs everywhere
It's there for all to see
And of course a damp-proof course
Would be a remedy
But this could prove expensive
And so we have to live
With fungus on the skirting boards
And plaster like a sieve!
Ill-fitting doors and windows…

Means draughts are common-place
Installing double glazing
Is something we can't face
The roof tiles are quite porous
Which means the loft is damp
And the wiring needs replacing
I've still got fifteen amp!
It's clear I have the attributes
To justify Grade II
And I'm part of our heritage
I'm proud of this – are you?"

A HARE RAISING EXPERIENCE

They said she was hare raising
What did that really mean?
An orphanage for leverets
Whose parents had been
Taken by a bird of prey
Or tried to cross the motorway
Leaving kids without protection
And vulnerable to early collection
By a passing dog or vixen
Once the fox had got a fix on
Scent that led straight to a meal
The threat from this source was quite real
Hare raising was a tough assignment
That required some realignment (of priorities)
Not something to be taken lightly
With many kids looking unsightly
And needing to be called to order
By those whose life-skills were much broader
So the hare raiser had striven
Reinforcing guide lines given
Creating a real sense of order
So that kids did not ignore her
And stray like parents now deceased
Becoming a predator's feast

OSCAR IN REVERSE

Oscar had a problem
His life was back to front
And sad to say some people
Thought it was just a stunt
To write a letter Oscar
Would start at bottom right
And he always had his breakfast
In the middle of the night
If he was in a restaurant
He'd want to pay the bill
Not when the meal was finished
But with consumption still at nil
Clothing was an issue
Shirts buttoned at the back
And reversing zips of any kind
Required a certain knack
His speech could be confusing
Since diction was affected
And he was hard to understand
Unless you had detected
That often he would talk to people
Starting at the finish
So for the vast majority
Clarity diminished…

So generally for Oscar
Life was quite a bind
When he started a new job
He'd already resigned
So poor old Oscar was perplexed
There wasn't a known cure
And he would live life back to front
Becoming less mature
The one thing that he did do
That was more help than not
He changed his name to Bob
And used it back to front a lot!

MOLLY OFF HER TROLLEY

Molly was a mature ewe
Not well known – you might ask who?
Since on the hillside, in the flock
She blended in with other stock
At shearing time she'd join the queue
Not pushing in like other ewes
But all this was due to change
For her behaviour became strange
This mature ewe whose name was Molly
Fell in love with a Tesco trolley!
As a sheep it must be said
Her shopping needs were limited
Occasional curlers for her coat
Bought jointly by both sheep and goats
A file to give her feet a treat
Linctus in case she lost her bleat
And spray to keep her sheep's breath sweet
And since she was of mature years
Products that allayed her fears
Of being rearranged as meat
Vacuum-packed, ready to eat
The trolley was parked near the gate
Said to be in a pristine state
The wheels worked well, they all ran true…

Not going sideways as some do
It seemed to be the perfect trolley
And this is what attracted Molly
Trolley love from the first meeting
Made clear by her excessive bleating
Infatuated by the cart
Which had deserted from the Mart
And now she found it hard to settle
Since falling for a lump of metal
Of course the trolley was inert
Did not respond to Molly's flirting
Which she found quite disconcerting
It was now a pathetic sight
Molly standing day and night
Losing weight – no appetite
A love-sick ewe with no insight
To help her to appreciate
The lack of response from her mate
Thankfully a van arrived
With Tesco painted on the side
A man got out, retrieved the trolley
Didn't give a thought to Molly
Who later on rejoined the flock
And blended in with other stock!

THE SNOWMAN

Only that morning he had walked
Across flat fields of green
But now, wrapped in a blanket
It was a different scene
Snow drifting at least to his waist
A blizzard had begun
The snowman's journey sapped his strength
The day would soon be done
Would he reach home by nightfall?
Would he stay at the helm?
The blizzard spoke "You will submit
My power will overwhelm"
The snowstorm now was so severe
It seemed he had to lose
But despite all he persevered
The ending *you must choose!*

LEGGING IT

Eric had a wooden leg
Nicely turned and with a peg
It used to be a kitchen table
Belonging to his Great Aunt Mabel
Ironically he'd hit a tree
When it was foggy and to see
The way ahead would have been hard
But even so he had been barred
From driving for a two-year spell
And he lost a leg as well
He managed well with just one leg
And didn't have to steal or beg
He had a steady occupation
As Porter at the Railway Station
Although when faced with trunks to carry
He'd quickly call his brother, Harry
Who also harboured an affliction
Which for the most part made his diction
Difficult to understand
In which case Eric lent a hand
Eric's leg was an antique
Getting older by the week
It had some superb patination
Admired by many at the station…

Eric clearly was quite proud
And often he would shout aloud
To anyone he thought should know
"It's been on the Antiques Road Show!"
His pride was hit early one morning
When he looked and without warning
Little holes came into view
The kind of holes woodworm would do
Harry, who could talk to woodworms
Stepped in to negotiate
Offered them a chest of drawers
To turn to dust – one they could eat
So Harry despite his poor diction
Came up trumps for his sibling
Saved his leg from this attack
To lose it would have been a sin
Now Eric's leg's back at the station
Proudly marching up and down
As shown on the Antiques Road Show
Woodworm free, the best in town!

NOT IN THE SWIM

Raymond, a rabbit of no fixed abode
Answered an advert placed by a toad
Who due to misfortune had lost all his money
And faced a future that didn't seem funny
The advert described a bedsit for let
All freshly painted, the best he'd seen yet
Raymond was desperate, he wanted to sign
"The sooner I do it, the place will be mine!"
But just as he started to sign for the room
Dark clouds above signalled rain through the gloom
The ingress of water into the room
Turning it into a watery tomb
And soon the water was up to the ceiling
Which understandably wasn't appealing
So better to live at no fixed abode
Than renting a bedsit designed for a toad!

THE SLIMMER

My figure's looking better
Than it has done for some time
For when I add the numbers up
There's an attractive bottom line
When I look in the mirror
I can't believe my eyes
My excess baggage disappeared
Around my arms and thighs
Now I am excited
When I go in a shop
I say "Is that in my size?"
And jaws no longer drop
Instead they fuss around me
Just like a VIP
And tell me just how good I look
Can this really be me?
But resting on your laurels
Can be a dangerous game
A week or two without control
Numbers don't stay the same
So if you're really serious
About losing weight
Remember you're responsible
You can't leave it to fate
And if you're striving for success
There is only one way
Control the food you eat
And exercise each day!

THE LONG JUMPER

Laurence was a long jumper
He stretched down to the knee
The person who had knitted him
Had done it carefully
With the Olympic games in mind
He tried to join the team
They asked him "are you track or field?"
And he said "I just dream"
He told them "I'm a long jumper
I'd say of some repute"
But they said "sorry we'll say no
Although you do seem cute
You see to join the British team
You wouldn't qualify
It appears that you've been knitted
And you're sheepish that is why
So even if you can jump far
The problem still remains
Construction is not skin and bone
With blood inside your veins
While a knitted jumper
Would offer an addition
Your wooliness just rules you out
By your own admission
So please don't get hysterical
Because of our rejection
If we do change our criteria
We'll consider your selection"

DELE – GATE

David couldn't delegate
To Deidre or to Don
Or in fact to anyone
In his team whereupon
They all got together
To discuss the issue more
Since David hogged the lot
The bottleneck was at his door
At the centre of the problem
Was David's inclination
To think he'd do a better job
Avoiding altercation
With those for whom the work was done
But his rationale was flawed
Because he did it all himself
The timing got ignored
Because he held on far too long
To things he should let go
His team was under utilised
And of course this would show
In a lack of motivation
Capability constrained
Frequent blind compliance
While David held the reins…

He failed to see that delegation
Wasn't an event
It needed careful planning
To ensure development
Once he understood this
He said "we'll have a go
And if I plan this properly
The benefits will show
My team will be more competent
Morale will increase too
And I can focus on the job
I'm really paid to do!"

DRIVEN TO DISTRACTION

Muriel was a strident ewe
Known by all, except a few
Since on the hillside in the flock
She didn't blend with other stock
At shearing time she'd jump the queue
Precisely what she shouldn't do
Unlike the more compliant ones
Who rarely spiked the sheep dogs' guns
She'd never do the sheep dogs' bidding
When challenged she'd say "are you kidding?"
Muriel liked to shop in town
Though local people often frowned
Because her driving was appalling
Not least because she kept on stalling
At roundabouts and at junctions
Not knowing how a gear box functions
Bunny hopping without stopping
In pursuit of her week's shopping
Was she crazy? Some would say so
Given her unique "stop, then go"
When at last she was barred
Her shopping trips could have been marred
But then she used a taxi firm
Whenever she required a perm…

Or to purchase sheepish make-up
A must to ensure top ram take-up
She'd often say her purse was lost
And seemed oblivious to the cost
Of trips to and round the town
Bills that made the farmer frown
For she expected him to pay
He did, but then on market day
She found herself put up for sale
Her spending was beyond the pale
And unlike the other sheep
Muriel was too dear to keep!

SIMPLY PERPLEXED

Poor Harold didn't know
Was he a zebra or a horse?
And since he was an orphan
Nobody could endorse
His origins and make him feel
Content with parentage
Consulting genealogists
Although it's all the rage
Did nothing to alleviate
Or indeed assuage
One day when he was galloping
Around the lower field
He put the brakes on sharply
When confronted, forced to yield
By a rather large pink elephant
Acquainted with his fate
Who said that he could empathise
And started to relate
His own story of ancestry
Over which there was debate
He explained how being pink
He wasn't "one of us"
And people often stared at him
On trains or on a bus...

Some folk would come up to him
And say "you should be grey"
And even worse were other folk
Who turned the other way
Pink was not a colour that they recognised
And it was so much easier
To avert their eyes
So he said I spend my time
Just trying to be me
It doesn't matter what you are
It's who you are that's key!
Afterwards young Harold said
"You've helped me quite a lot
I'll concentrate on who I am
And forget about the what!"

"TAKE A RISK, BUY AN OBELISK!"

It stands resplendent by the lawn
Pushing skyward to adorn
A piece of the external space
Tasteful and not 'in your face'
It took some time and careful thought
Initial ideas came to nought
Gormley's Angel too intrusive
Neighbours had been quite abusive
Didn't like the patination
On this particular creation
Then we considered Blackpool Tower
Reaction locally was sour
Writing in the village news
Most who wrote did not enthuse
Who cares what other people say
We'll buy an obelisk today
Ideal for that garden corner
Better than hot tub or sauna
Our neighbours now don't speak to us
Our obelisk caused quite a fuss!

THE SPY AT NIGHT

Once I met a man called Ray
A hospital porter by day
By night he worked for MI6
He told me his code name was X
Many found it quite surprising
That he was so enterprising
Though one could say he's suave and charming
With a manner that's disarming
Sadly this just wasn't true
Lacked sophistication too
Before you criticise old Ray
Take care for he could win the day
For it seems that in the night
He became quite erudite
His use of language was impressive
Though anecdotes some thought excessive
Crosswords kept his brain in trim
Rather like a mental gym
He'd always be in bed by ten
Picked up his assignment then
Often tackled secret missions
Involving dangerous conditions
This time he had to crack the code
An intellectual episode…

An enigma variation
Only Ray could save the nation
It was a race against the clock
The prize the code he would unlock
For he knew that when he woke
He'd be an ordinary bloke
A hospital porter by day
A routine job with little pay
But for Ray it didn't matter
A patient's smile enough to flatter!

TREE STUMPED

The woodpecker said "I am stumped
It feels just like being gazumped
I paid in advance for this tree
The Agent did seem fair to me
I said I'd sign when I got back
Not thinking squirrels would attack
But while I went to get my bags
Two squirrels who were both old lags
Caught the Agent on the hop
Saying that they could not stop
But if he'd take a double fee
They'd sign the form immediately
They wanted to move in 'today'
In other words move straight away
And by the time that I got back
They'd even had time to unpack
They looked at home in what I thought
Was the tree-hole I had bought
I guess the thing that I have learned
Having got my fingers burned
Is to sign first, then get my bags
Or risk defeat by two old lags!"

BEING 40

Old enough to have acquired wisdom
Young enough to look forward to the many
years ahead

Old enough to have faced many challenges and
learned from them
Young enough to look forward to challenges in
the future

Old enough to recognise that success comes in
many different forms
Young enough to pursue success on your terms

Old enough to recognise the balance which is
right for you between family and career
Young enough to pursue both with enthusiasm

Able to recognise the important things in life

All the above at 40!

TEMPUS FUGIT – DON'T ABUSE IT!

"I haven't got the time" he said
So how much have you got?
"About the same as all the rest
My opening line was just in jest
Or to be honest – an excuse
For letting time out on the loose
Not even on a piece of string
So if I need to reel it in
I could at least pull something back
But with no string I'm on the rack
I really should prioritise
And get this time thing down to size
Since I am regularly afflicted
I don't achieve what I've predicted
Optimism fills my eyes
But then things don't materialise
Good timing always holds the key
To living life effectively!"

RUNNER BEAN

Freddie had a runner bean
Training hard all season
But didn't make the British team
Was not given a reason
All agreed he had the speed
The fastest bean around
They offered him the pole vault
But Freddie only frowned
Selectors had met earlier
And rapidly concluded
That pole vaulting was right for him
But running was excluded
Being a competitor
Our bean launched an appeal
He hoped to meet selectors
And maybe do a deal
Sadly the Lawyer he had hired
Had now moved abroad
Replacing him was difficult
Since Lawyers' fees had soared
At last a date for his appeal
Came through so not yet beaten
But before the case was heard
We're told…
Poor Freddie had been eaten!

MOON WALKING

Once I had a pet baboon
Who fancied travelling to the moon
I explained "It's far away"
"Can't I do it in a day?"
Said the baboon and was upset
Encouragement he did not get
The baboon said "Give up – no way
I'm going to do it anyway"
First he bought some hiking boots
And climbing gear with maps and routes
Until he was all kitted out
And well prepared, there was no doubt
"Via India's the route I'll try
For some of it is in the sky
It looks like Everest is best"
Though somewhat glazed he now expressed
"I aim to be the first baboon
To set foot upon the moon"
He made good progress to the top
But found that there was no bus stop
No trams, no trains, no motorway
To take him to the moon that day
And of course there was no bus
Nor was there a terminus…

The infrastructure was not there
So the baboon had to declare
"I'll give up my quest just now
Unless I can travel by cow
I've heard that cows are superfit
And can jump right over it"
He was in luck, a cow appeared
And having listened volunteered
To take him to the moon and back
Strapped on his back, inside a sack
"You must wear goggles" said the cow
"The wind chill factor's strong just now"
The baboon travelled there and back
The first to travel in a sack
With applause from everyone
He now plans to go to the sun!

SHOOTALINUS
AND THE TRAPPINGS OF SUCCESS

His name was Shootalinus
He was a ticket tout
Based at the Colosseum
When Romans were about
He rendered unto Caesar
As little as he could
For lining his own pocket
Was what he understood
He'd plenty of back-handers
For favouring the few
And making sure, during a show
That they got a good view
His network, it was legion
He knew a lot of folk
He seemed to be quite popular
Amongst arena blokes
So he could spare a victim
If someone tipped the wink
To get a prisoner back alive
Was easier than you'd think
Eventually his downfall
Came because of his success
Spotted by a Senator
Who said "You're overdressed…

Clearly you're Plebeian
And shouldn't dress that way
I think you are nefarious
It's fortunate – today
I'm one short on the programme
For which the crowd has paid"
The tout now started shivering
Clearly he was afraid
He fumbled in his pocket
For his mobile – not yet made
The Senator said "You're in luck
Your session won't take long
You're in with the lions
They've been hungry for too long"
So Shootalinus knew
That given what was said
The one thing that was certain
Was that he would soon be dead!

Shootalinus now in chains
With other star attractions
Was taken to the Green Room
All present, no subtractions
Cheek by jowl with other 'guests'
All locked up safe and sound
Beneath the great arena
His heart began to pound
On Wednesday there were chat shows
But this was Saturday!

And something more spectacular
Was needed on this day
Since the audiences paid double
At the weekend, so they say
The Senator who ran the show
Acted as MC
Announcing acts in sequence
As per programme usually
But breaking with convention
He told the crowd "today
We're fortunate to offer
A colourful display
By Shootalinus – ticket tout
Who's free just for today"
While all this was happening
The tout thought on his feet
Could he persuade the lions
That he wasn't good to eat?

A short course in hypnosis
Offered in Green Room Two
Given his predicament
Could prove useful to do
Having grasped the basics
The rudimentary skills
He joined 'guests' in the tunnel
Where they were given pills
To make them all more fearless
In the face of opposition…

Since lions had the upper hand
And were in good condition
Finally the whistle blew
They entered the arena
And they remarked the other side
Looked leaner and much meaner
The ticket tout looked confident
After the Green Room training
But confidence can be misplaced
Then there's no point complaining
It cost him an arm and a leg
Disabled his finances
What's more, to go out on a limb
Had not improved his chances
A lion charged and cut him down
Destroyed his useless lance
The hypnotist was just a fraud
The tout paid in advance
Afterwards a friend of his
Lamented his demise
"Nobody tipped the wink" he said
"The sun was in our eyes"
To promise prisoners freedom
On payment was a con
Shootalinus knew this, whereupon
He went and tried the hypnotist
What else could he do?
Poetic justice in the end –
Since he had been conned too!